mucha
muchacha
too much girl

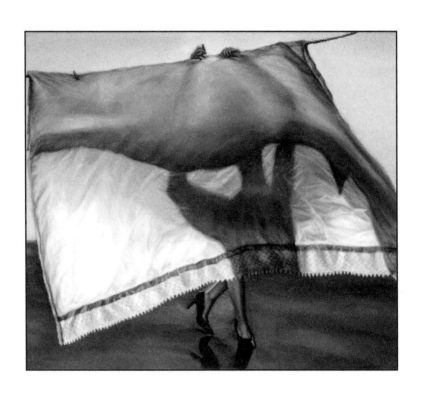

mucha muchacha
too much girl

POEMS

Leticia Hernández-Linares

TIA CHUCHA PRESS

ISBN: 978-1-882688-51-7

Book Design: Jane Brunette
Cover art: "Hold the Line" by Ana Teresa Fernández
Back cover photo: Michelle Gutiérrez

Published by:
Tía Chucha Press
A Project of Tía Chucha's Centro Cultural, Inc.
PO Box 328
San Fernando, CA 91341
www.tiachucha.org

Distributed by:
Northwestern University Press
Chicago Distribution Center
11030 South Langley Avenue
Chicago IL 60628

Tía Chucha's Centro Cultural & Bookstore is a 501 (c) 3 nonprofit corporation funded in part over the years by the National Endowment for the Arts, California Arts Council, Los Angeles County Arts Commission, Los Angeles Department of Cultural Affairs, The California Community Foundation, the Annenberg Foundation, the Weingart Foundation, the Lia Fund, National Association of Latino Arts and Culture, Ford Foundation, MetLife, Southwest Airlines, the Andy Warhol Foundation for the Visual Arts, the Thrill Hill Foundation, the Middleton Foundation, Center for Cultural Innovation, John Irvine Foundation, Not Just Us Foundation, the Attias Family Foundation, and the Guacamole Fund, among others. Donations have also come from Bruce Springsteen, John Densmore of The Doors, Jackson Browne, Lou Adler, Richard Foos, Gary Stewart, Charles Wright, Adrienne Rich, Tom Hayden, Dave Marsh, Jack Kornfield, Jesus Trevino, David Sandoval, Denise Chávez and John Randall of the Border Book Festival, Luis & Trini Rodríguez, and others.

contents

MI GENTE (¡USTEDES!)

For Mama, 93 years strong
and for all
las Mucha Muchachas

Te vas Alfonsina con tu soledad
¿Qué poemas nuevos fuíste a buscar?
Una voz antigua de viento y de sal
te requiebra el alma y la está llevando
y te vas hacia allá como en sueños
dormida, Alfonsina vestida de mar.

SUNG BY MERCEDES SOSA
WRITTEN BY
FÉLIX LUNA & ARIEL RÁMIREZ

comadre

1

Soy una mujer hecha de palabras
Desde la antigüedad
Mi sangre flotó en la sopa de letras
Del vientre de mi madre

GIOCONDA BELLI

Underneath the Cuento

I count the story because to tell is to count
like numbering splotches on skin, having to interpret
layers of wrinkles that now camouflage them.
Te voy a contar un cuento.

Splotches on skin interpret and
keep time with the story she is going to tell you.
Te voy a contar un cuento.
It requires you breathe on a lower register.

The story she is going to tell you sinks in time.
You try to hold most of it, try to cut parts out.
Your breath dropping to a lower register will reason
if underneath is low and the bass is the lowest note,
then the bajo will play a good rhythm.

The story is counted because to tell is to count.

1. Her husband will not have spit out pieces of
her devotion by the door before
he slammed it. Me voy.

2. A black and white photograph of a husband and wife
in a peeling gold frame will not sit on her dresser fifty years
and many deaths later. Same dresser.

3. She will not have bandaged desperate hands
in starless Hollywood apartments with the crinkled dollars
she scrubbed for in two story Pasadena
homes. A mother's love.

4. Her oldest son will not spin the cylinder,
will not lose to roulette. Two out of three.

A good song rips the roots up from a telling
so you can move and hum the melodious edges,
only repeat the honeyed notes,
like Donny singing the song right to you.

Move, hum the edges melodious and off tune
until the order of things dance in your memory.
Tear the pages out, but don't bury them until
you sing the words right for you.

1. I met him crumpled under hospital linens, trying to die,
small man who left big wounds. ¿Te vas?

2. All the male copies of his face crumbled
under the weight, so I wonder
if bones lowered into the ground
can make good canes. Better we limp.

3. Everyone is asleep but no one is resting,
and I keep going home.

4. The echo of so many footsteps
push me to keep marching.

Te voy a contar un cuento.
The story that she tells you
good for swaying to sleep.
But mine makes you hum
until you lose your breath.

Learning to Talk

I learned to talk sin pelos en la lengua
saying that literally means
without hair on one's tongue
suggesting a sense of speaking
without reservation

I learned to talk
en letras
que no tienen forma,
formless letters, pronouns foreign
in English, in Spanish, singing
for a family learning to walk

with tongues made
of metal, of mud.

Faces blurry framed by static in two languages
first remembrance at five, a dream
about waking, waking to sirens, somebody's crying,
Little Red Hiding Hood skipping through the barrio.
You can find your way home
by the markers of mispronounced stories.
La Caperucita Roja ask-ed the wolf.
Mami, así no se dice.

You can find your way home
by markers like the rusty
car carcasses surrounded by weeds
holding up old-school cholos

leaning on promises of fleeing,
the tunnel filtering drops of light,
hum of exhaust, rhythm of rubber
spinning Hollywood Freeway medleys.
Here, I learn to talk
somewhere between comb in back pocket,
feathered hair liberty,
big wings will fly me away from Joe, where he's goin'
with that gun, fly me far from the Pusher Man
who tapped my uncle too hard, and orange leaves
hanging from the torn chair,
tying his tongue

What's your first   language?
no, your first   language,
so you're truly bilingual   what language
do you dream in?

I dream in black and white like letters splattered
on my father's chest, a t-shirt he bought
"If you liked Vietnam, you're going to love El Salvador"
I dream in Hail Mary men are in the driveway,
the walls covered with muffled warnings.
We will need grace. Hard knocks at the door
bring pieces of English
brother dead sorry
on the wall feathers tied to circles
are not armed to deal
with muertos this heavy.

She says maybe it's the poetry
the going back hurts, can't you write
something happy.

If you abridge my version, my melody
goes flat, see I never made it
to chola, so caught up in rock,
pop, new wave, stopped at cha cha
fill in the bubbles, all of the above,
my father didn't believe
in God, solamente en la música.

Can you feel   can you feel
can you feel the beat within my heart
bouncing off my body
dragging dreamscapes weighing me down,
sabes que, it starts with my sex.
In the heart and darkness of learning
to be female no pain was no gain raised
as a tragic lady you don't know happy
it has to hurt to mean something.

These letters spin by heart,
break down the broken historical
record, pantomime the past, piece
threads into transparent textile

at the crossroads between my split
tongue, points of unknown origin,
Eleguá, receives the song I leave
for him to untangle.

iba o iba orisha
a laroye moforibale
iba o iba orisha

Too Much Girl

1.
Tiptoeing around lines
sharp with analytical points, the scholar
stuffs his anger into discourse.

The map that led to graduate school
catapults me into a blank space.
No precedent, I seek anchor
in man-made green fields and old bells.

The town sign reads: thickly settled.
A nestled entitlement here breaks
the asphalt up to suit its inhabitants.
This brick academy was built
to prepare white men to run things,
not counting on me. I find a chair,
later, a skunk.

I read Fanon who painted the situation
of the native as nervous,
furiously across rough pages
his tempest of words clamors, finally
explanations about the damage
graphed onto my cells.

The reporter from *The Globe* writes me
into a slum, lifts me out of my shoes,
barefoot is how he likes me. Afraid to turn doors
without permission,

once I open them, they keep swinging,
back and forth.

2.
But is a door a door
define door,
unhinge it, pour microscopic lenses over the grain,
find the core, until there is no more door.

3.
I am the native observing the experiments:
windowsills a stage for jars full of bees
with broken stingers,
a fantastic golden mass of grating
against my solemnity.
You laugh. When your expression tires, let me
show you the survival rates.

I took a job building pantheons for those
who enter through the ivory
and don't return. My back bends
under the unscripted chronicle,
a continued condition of disquiet.

Lumps on my hands—skin blossoms, symptoms
of my state sprout ganglions, that
strange flower disrupting movement,
scrambling messages. A fantastic golden mass
of buzzing inside my hands.

My joints succumb. Elder mothers hover
at the table where I am covered in needles
trying to push through blockages that keep
my hands still.

4.
Define body,
dislocate, pour microscopic lenses
over its legibility outside
of parodies and ironies until
there is nobody.

5.
The elder's wrinkled hands hold white gauze
over the slivers in my palms. The doctor
in my heart pleads for me
to confess. I am present in a building
that I could not enter once. Doorknobs
taunt me, stick—and my weak hands.

The professor, blonde bun at her neck, slams
the gavel on the short brown girl's head.
The specimen has an amazing acumen,
she should be studied. Another professor proclaims
the short brown girl is unable to theorize upon
the literature by a skinny over-privileged man
who questions existence, discards it in his boredom.
There is, gentlemen, no subject, since there is no one
left to conquer.

6.
Tune the chord,
delineate it as vocal, lubricate
the entry, practice the lyrics out loud, until
everyone can hear you.

7.
My mother used to cut the muscle into squares,
immerse an untied tongue in tomate y caldo.
We eat lengua and don't ask whose words
should swim in the broth. My restless verbage,
a missing ingredient. Y, a esta qué le pasó,
didn't anyone explain to her. My resistant questions
pushing against the absurdity
of a people who eat their own tongue.

Amor en el tiempo boca abajo

1.
The first notes of our long play romance
travel through signal and cable.
His morning call delivers unexpected news,
airplanes burnt clouds down to their innards.
Night pulled itself over morning.

Fragments of the globe and the towers
jigsaw first and third worlds, workers
on the same block, dead under same rubble.
Mourning for safe secure never happen here.
I gargle with I told-you-so.

This love song is doomed to fail. Journalism
compels my attention, a professor's podium
demands your deconstruction.
Before, you wrote notes on licorice root,
painted me a word temple
over telephone wire for paper.
What if we write, and we write it away.

2.
Stones slip like dominoes under dutiful
pilgrimage on sun pyramid. We salute Popocatepetl,
smoking mountain, filling the sky with burning towers.

Iztaccihuatl, mujer durmiendo, sometimes snow
falling over her, presides over souls reaching for blankets,
bodies cold under buildings folding, stacking like cards.

Sliver of moon from any vantage is a woman
rolled into her own womb, weeping
the world into water again.

3.
Later, we arrive at the resort, welcomed
by hands open for the weight of la propina:
for water, for air, nothing is exempt.

The infinity pool divides salt and chlorine,
blurs the wave of caminantes en las calles,
the cop's venomous finger signaling us to the curb
for looking like we do, being where we are.

4.
Ready to write together in historic bars
and play long suites on vinyl, you are skeptical
about how this is a love poem.
Brazen under the barbarians that govern us,
we sculpt a heartbeat, compose refrains for the farce.

This song between us, this chorus
streaming from the eyes of la gente,
is like a chant from all mouths,
the wish from the hands
of a people hambrienta.

We pull live stems
from among lacerated longing limbs,
fill grasping hands with the red velvet kiss
of justice that assures when pulverized
and splintered down to a grey powder,
we are all finally the same.

Holy Mother

Dusting seconds
off fast clocks, she coughs,
the *what ifs* that linger
like big pieces of cotton, bits
of leaves from a cigar.
Ceremony's requisite
is to release the weight
of children left behind,
the burials
of their sacred hearts.

Of combustible tierra,
open mouthed peaks,
igneous traces stamp her skin.
A hint of ash. Left El Salvador
seeking salve and bandage—anxious
expressions in the rearview.
No time to mourn her bleeding.

The mechanics to bear, or not,
severed things overpower grief.
Her blood in exile, fraying hems
holding the present together.

Hija, yo no tuve tiempo
por la menopausia,
is what she said, maybe
she was laughing.

On to another page.
Yellow lights recalling
Saturdays at El Moctezuma
when she demanded every eye.
Marco Antonio Muñiz corroborates
on warped vinyl.

In pursuit of a dance,
a refill of relentless
moisture, of tropical scent.
Rounds fading the missing, the pieces.
Ice cube refrains interrupt holy mother
routine—stand-in, keeper
of someone else's children.

Así es hija. We would leave
la Virgencita to protect all
we had of them—fading images,
while we took swigs to abate separation,
humming along to "El Tamarindo"
and the hard truths de Los Panchos.

Her recollection cradles
my daydream of riding waterfalls
powered by all the tears
she tells me at 82 she regrets.
Not for a man, not for anyone.

In my version, no one drowns,
no one gets trapped
in a Maria-Félix-red-lipstick-
dramatic-movie-title kind of

way, under delayed dreams disappearing,
in the static symbol of the Virgin Mary.

So, did la Virgen
go through menopause?
Girl, she didn't even have sex.

How to be Spiritual in Stilettos

With the desire to tower
as many inches as possible
above short and round, she squeezes
ten swollen toes into a too narrow, leather, and
pointy hold.

Wholly spiritual, we want to see
from new levels. Tacones
allow us to scrape the sky.
Taconazos our multi-use
ammunition. Hitting concrete
in unison, marching
clickety clack
all the way to confession.

Intricate liturgy of alteration,
but part of a little girl's
madness, the sparkle of a glossy footprint
first unearthed from a tree trunk.
Pencil thin pedestal contests
a kitten heel selling grace—so many
inches closer to the forbidden panorama.

Under fluorescent skylights, the maze
of an endless aisle, bright red Dorothy
slippers nudge me, promise rainbows,
someday. At the check stand, I hand over
cash for size six little girl wishes
in the form of pocket-sized shoes
molded from red glitter into hopeful.

Porque no todos somos iguales

X is for xochitl, wilting burnt orange petals
stand at attention, guarding graves
in Tapachula, guiding the way for disappeared
migrants who, buried penniless in unmarked coffins,
are on their way to get their names back.

X fills in the blank of letras desaparecidas
of the son who went to join his mother,
the daughter who went to work for her brother,
the family members packed into buses
spanning the road to cross the OTM,
Other Than Mexican, border.

Dos equis is etched on lonely wood slabs
no one claims, no one visits.
Here lies fulano de tal:
salvadoreño, guatemalteca, hondureño,
unidentified Central American, the casualty
marked by two sticks forming a cross.

X is greater than the number
of Central Americans disappeared
in civil wars. Spoils at end of conflict
wear an old visage, include a destination.
But before you pass go, you have to dance
with ghosts, wade through reluctant rivers,
evade jungle foliage, ruthless train tracks hunting
for limbs, coyotes, and policías riding seesaws.

Lucía Elizabeth Contreras encontró
a su hermano en la foto—by his shirt.
Lucky, not like la mujer whose extremities
distribute like milagros on a Tapachula altar
stamped, plated by locomotion, brown
copper-colored. Tracks juggled her parts
but spared her from mass graves
where bodies hope and wait for someone
to please bring them a name.

Tamal stands lining Macarthur Park under blue
and white awnings de El Salvador, de Guatemala.
The letters and flags look the same. Men on corners
hold invisible cards between thumb and index.
Offers for identification still unverified.

First you have to get here.
No one agrees on numbers. 25,000
over many years, 80,000 just in one.
Zeros above rising temperature turbulent
ocean tides washing up Salvadorans in México.
They emerge with the taste of new anthems
rinsing the vos out of their mouths.

Un primo me ofrece sentar, compa' hazme
compañía, y te cuento. Hours later labels peel
under drops of bottle sweat, we swallow tears
in gulps of liquid bread. Dos equis, two x or maybe
its Pilsner, Pacífica without the label—hard to tell.

I sign epigraphs in as many letters as I can,
pero sin nombre. I traded them for la muerta's pink
rosary bursting under pressure, beads disbursing pleas.

Don't need bubblegum prayers, she scoffed and took me
to dance, asking after origins. From never never
land, never a land of the living, crowded
by dehydrated spirits looking for a name tag?

Parched for an alphabet without the letters
o t m or x, regateando las letras estoy,
to buy train tickets home for the dead.

Tragedilandia

People refuse red lights,
dismiss cars, and waves
of bodies feed a hungry calle—
the Mission's pulse.

Raising eyebrows, viejos consider
yesterday's residue, how reluctant
the morning rouses to youngsters
holding pamphlets, blasting beliefs
into bullhorns—hurry up, save your souls.

Between numbered blocks, the hole in the wall
tienda is open, shelves skinny, like counters
wedged between front porches
and the street, with just a little bit
of a few things, en las colonias, back home.

On Mission, Julio's wall-to-wall knick knacks
spray cumbias along the walk
to Panchita's restaurant servings of a certain vos,
fijate, way of saying things.

Familiar stream of greetings deflated,
as reporters use up all the words:
tragedia/centroamérica/noticias/después.

News reports count numbers with too many zeros.
Count bodies, moving land, bodies, broken
houses, bodies.

Exhumations unveil letters in the cracked earth,
spelling out an indignation buried
in generations de olvido.

Our dead, still to be sorted, lie under fresh mounds
of greed, new building plans piling
on top of them. El Salvador's bolero
of shaking window, rattling crater cradles
63,000 plus houses trading for pieces of roof.

Little men stand tall, draw up plans using erasers.
The earth didn't just move, it went in reverse.

Yo vengo de la tierra,
la tierra de tragedia,
yo vengo de la tierra,
la tierra de tragedia
El Salvador, no se salvó,
el país que hasta Dios olvidó

I sing melancholy verses about
a prostrate land eating its own offspring,
and suddenly I want to be dramatic,
pull my hair back tight, say the word
"tragedia," sexy, so you'll like it and want more.

Welcome to Tragedilandia, we've got it all:
massacre, earthquake, hurricane,
civil war, massacre again, but the women
and children first please, earthquake again...

In this farce, red paints my lips in a smile
so I can laugh and dance for you,

like the clown El Chocolate—pervert payaso
who used to wander my father's
vecindad in search of grace and inhibition.

More of a smile-now-cry-sooner-than-later clown,
not feeling very sexy, I smear
color from my mouth, watch scant news coverage.
Desperate for outcry about my family's
country, my father's ramblings remind me,
through his rants, phrases falling out
like dust you can't sweep away
Salvadorans are like cucas.
Keep coming back and we're everywhere.

Translating the Wash

The lady who washes what
the neighborhood wears
doesn't pretend to like you,
so when she asks where
my clean clothes will travel,
she really wants to know.

El Salvador, my parent's country,
registers no recognition.
Offering a pen and interest,
she urges a drawing
on the back of an already
opened envelope.

Her expression doesn't follow
the tiny dots and hasty marks
I ink on the paper. Central America
below Mexico, the longitude
graphs itself around us.

Vietnamese sputters
from the twenty-something-year-old
radio without an antenna saving us
from an awkward silence.

Maybe if I say the country
is not too different
from her Vietnam—a thought
that makes a hole

in the counter, filling with sand,
the comparison muddled before translation.

Fifteen years and only a terminally
vacant apartment, a church
she can't pray in but that she worships
outside her window,
she has sewn my ripped fabric
together, erased stains, polished delicates.
Always open, except Sundays and holidays.

The cut and color of my clothing change
over fifteen years, and she wraps
safe travel wishes in plastic,
congratulating me on my births, describing
her father's death—first trip back home.

A long stretch between visits,
I bring her my post-maternity
pants to hem and a newborn.
His bouncy bare feet
unearth laughter, tender confession,
jagged-edged warnings from her.

No children, because she didn't have
enough money. This business—her child.
Wondering about me just this morning,
inquires after my first born. Sends me away
with a promise of shorter pants and relief
that the older one is not just crazy.

In her hometown, a little girl was so mad
at the baby her mother brought home,

she yelled her dissatisfaction
out the window—jumped out after it.
Just crazy. Probably better with boys.

I pack her story in my bag, wait and wish
for shock, dismay, but they don't come.
Some things are not lost in translation.

I try to send her customers,
but her refusal to feign
contentment with the folding of days
between other people's creases
scares them away.

Tired of giving directions at the coordinates
that mark an immigrant woman's arrival
and where she finds bread and breath,
I don't bother to translate.

Sweat

We're not gonna go on a trip glorifying the pava
which is a straw hat, or the guayabera
which is a type of shirt, cause there ain't no hat
or no shirt gonna free anybody.
　　　　　—Juan Sánchez

Sewing machines whirr in unison,
bruise the auditory surround
like the successive tap of typewriter keys,
just one word written over and over.
Stories stitched under seams
hang in the air waiting to be told.
Scraps of letters written
to no one in particular
collect dust on the fábrica floor.

Writing her life on a hem line, Hilda watches
for shifts in the light. Windows are the choked up
holes that don't let the sun through anymore,
in the old garage where rusted tables,
tired sewing machines breathe heavily.
As the day slowly advances, Hilda gets anxious
for the view she's missing of overcast sky and the smog.

Querido: Las agujas me sacan sangre de los dedos
pequeños y cada día menos femeninos, más torcidos
aún así….¿me seguirás queriendo?
Las agujas le escriben cartas al destino
sobre líneas hechas de hilo.

Lupe wipes the narrative running across her forehead,
sews S.O.S. messages in bold colors
that will imprint themselves on a young girl's back
on an afternoon when wet air blends
with cotton, polyester, sweat. A tag sticking to her skin
reads size seven even though it's really size one.
Pant legs that fight her thighs and don't
accommodate her thickness are flags.

Made in El Salvador
Made in Taiwan
Made by my tía
Made by una niña
Made in T.J.
Made in L.A.
Made by a slave

Leaning over a cracked sheet of wood,
Hilda, Betina, and Rosa follow Betsy Ross's example.
Except without the rocking chairs and exhibits displaying
charcoal silhouettes of factory owners, antique artifacts
from sweatshops, impressionistic renditions of stale air,
clay molds of empty hands.

Sewing for their lives, they fabricate flags,
tiny hoochie shirts in red, blue, white.
Their discarded countries are pieces of the past
that they throw out at the end of an endless day,
when the crooked door stops letting light through.
Offerings in silk, cotton blue left in the dark under
skeptical sewing tables read:

querida santita de la fábrica please
let me trade my m-a-i-d for a m-a-d-e
in the U.S.A label. Packing the sun into her bag,
Hilda looks forward to citizenship exam prep
for dinner. Faint melodies of Salvadoran
national anthem scorching the bottom of her pans.
Hilda lines them with study questions, written on foil.

Just can't wait
to be 'an American city,'
as she likes to say,

and have a new flag
to put into the flames.

Cumbia de salvación

Cumbia sabrosa cumbia, para ti yo bailo hasta el amanecer

Legs wrap around each other
es la culpa del verso,
on the floor, wood lodges
in the skin open at our heels.

Caderas to the right, to the left
hips swing swaying to el acordeón
hitting notes to the side.

What it is that en realidad
manda en mi país, no es,
el ritmo sabrosón del Salvador.
Es el peso, el dólar, el colón.
Paper currency o cualquier tipo
de intercambio.

Pedacitos of broken bone
splinter in our teeth. Spitting them out,
we count steps, sweep soreness
from the joints—wish I could say
oh, the dancing. Tired arms
scour the greed from resistant corners.

Watch my curves cut through the cadence
of my babosada spree at el 99.
I request all parts of the animal,

wrap red juice of tripa in new dish towels.
Are you watching? As I make deals
that keep me scrubbing to meet
the minimum on the statement.

Try to stack under my pillow
so when I visit I can dance
under neon duty free sign,
binge on brand names
sport a striped American feel.

Pa pa ra pa cu cu cumbia
Yes girl, it's the remix,
not the record scratched
or skipping. Repetition
but of choreography, interpreting
where desire and wallet part ways.
Sellers nodding heads, unfolding welcome
mats—sold, for cheap.

Es dinero el que manda en mi país
Es el ritmo sabrosón del Salvador

Para allá para acá ay para qué,
did you hear about la fulanita,
out of work, never goes dancing
¿Y eso? es que she danced
right into the store, slipped and fell
on her debt.

Cumbia de mis amores

Diamond Girl y La Spazz

Cassette tape ribbons unravel a wisdom,
La Diamond Girl y la Spazz swear Stevie B
and Keith Sweat, hold the secrets of their hearts.

The lyrics testify to the high school petitions
for a cute guy to notice, once peroxide
finishes running through her hair to unveil
a blonde mane, fading the black,
in the absence of marble-colored eyes,
maybe gold hair will show the sparkle.

The tatted white guy who married a Mayan
woman, despite their mismatched language
points out orange tinted tresses, burnt color
like grease accumulating under cuts
of meat frying, accuses her of looking
like she's in a gang, honestly wants to know
what did she do to her hair.

Too little chola, too much clown, like the one
on his arm laughing loud at la Spazz,
humming Stevie B, but substituting new words:
Zanahoria girl, Zanahoria girl
trying for Charlie's Angels, she ended up
looking like una cualquiera, a carrot-head,
facing endless layers of bad orange hair days.

La Zanahoria girl crisps straight strands
into crimps and curls, teases the round into length,
to lessen the fullness of her cheeks, didn't
the commercials promise yellow swirls?
Ay niña, that's for the white girls.
Diamond Girl breaks down princess hair,
for the locks that make all the boys feel,
all the boys dream—you have to use bleach.

Cha-cha mixtape ribbon tying together wishes
for a skinny hairless appearance, tangles
in the player. Girls donning pink toenails
that fit into floppy mesh plastic shoes
from Zody's, disco bunny just another phase
like heavy metal, new wave
flip through glossy magazine pages,
anticipation in their chests.

Mucha muchacha

Mucha Mu-cha-cha

Busy hands collect nine lives,
religious trinkets, mark each act
of the play trying to bury her
with translucence and saint names.
Zoraida's rings bang an anxious entreaty
back and forth over dusty surfaces.

Mucha Mu-cha-cha

Waking old under the city's
respiratory system, she inhales a quiet
daybreak. No feet shuffling, no smell
of a man's clothes. Rubbing brass
Buddha's belly, she mutters prayers
under dimly lit statues, sends telegrams
on barbed paper. The bare minimum—just
enough money, at some point, salvation.

Mucha Mu-cha-cha

Zoraida fills the empty spaces with invitados.
Hips and elbows crowd into a tiny house.
Carcajadas spilling over, arms extended.

Mucha Mu-cha-cha

Gossip wedges thick under heels
gathering around little story appetizers,

liquored sweet confessions. Esa Pilar holds
court, draws a red heart around
her gap-toothed smile, packs her purse
with details about fulanitas, y no
lo van a creer.

Blue trimmed envelopes, sides torn open pour
bomb stained skies out, adorn the morning bus ride
as Zoraida digs q-tips into loyal lipstick
tubes she can't bear to discard.

Back home, money, marriage, a house
with solid walls, anything but
broke-ass-dirt-poor, you hire
a muchacha, a girl to do your work.
'girl,' and 'work,' stick like nuégados en miel,
panela melted, smothering. Too much. Mucha
muchacha. It's just too much girl.

Facing each sunrise ready to lift herself, pull
children up by the collar, stand them before glass
promise of possible, Zoraida stores
skipped heartbeats, sacrificed yearning
into shoeboxes. Too much, too much girl.

When the professor she used to clean for
attends granddaughter's graduation, laughter erupts
in her chest. Her cheekbones pop with possible blooming
with disappeared dignity dug up from the molten. Hands
blurred in continual applause as her girl dons cap, gown,
awards, sharp tongue. Professor, what do you know
about this mucha muchacha.

Mucha Mu-cha-cha,
it's just too much girl.

hija 2

Memory is never complete.
There are always parts of it that
time has amputated. Writing is a
way of retrieving them, of bringing
the missing parts back to it, of
making it more holistic.

Nawal El Saadawi

Shuco

Sunday morning ritual begins with an empty sand colored gourd
balancing on a straw ring. It awaits the gruel, gray

in our ears. La ropa sucia crowds our drinking, bits of grain
slide down the sides of our mouths. Shuco.

Another word for dirty. Shuco for the boys, sucia
for the girls. Always worse to be a dirty girl.

A hot sweet sludge, three black beans at the bottom, a lucky
Cracker Jack surprise. Where we come from, corn grows dark.

Lucky to escape a civil war, we invent our own
combat. Unclassified, our fatalities become residual.

We drink corn under the consequence of late night remember-whens,
after, no one grinds it. We open packages of dust for remedy,

mix them with water, in our transplanted kitchen. The swirl of hot
atol looking like cement—hard to translate. You can find it roadside,

at the top of a mountain, or in the cabinet. It's a quicksand.
This porridge subsumes the words she says shouldn't be wasted

on such nasty recuerdos. Yet, the tally grows long like her hair
of the missing. Así empieza mi cuento.

Sunday morning ritual soothes yesterday's transgressions
turned to mud in the gourd, balancing on a straw ring.

Looking for three black beans, bits of seed, Cracker Jack surprise, we scrape the dead from the bottom of the bowl.

La Cuchillera

El gallo didn't ring that morning. Unpaid long distance phone bills
left him disconnected, the dawn estranged from his echo.

Eager appetites waiting in the limbo between sky opening its eyes
y la madre levantándose, push Dolores out of bed.

Word skyscrapers rising, voices commuting, what's
for breakfast, did you iron my…Scribbled reminders
flapping in the wind, falling off tired tongues.
Counters cringe under stacks of notices making her hate
the mail carriers. Greedy envelopes bearing no benevolence,

only vengeful balances. Shut off dates menace, she admits
to her neighbor Estella, whose husband overindulges,
but at least he doesn't beat her.

Were Dolores to compose cumbias,
she would sing stubborn men strong, erase
complacent women in a chorus, glue
unpaid bills to the trunks of trees,
let weather, hungry insects reject the math.

Back home in Santa Ana, full moons rest
on the horizon like musical notes, crafting cantos
about women from el barrio, Santa Bárbara.

Cuchilleras, their feet moving with Changó.
Son de las que no se dejan.

Cuchillera, you
knife woman,
you will need this lesson
when your day begins and ends in a displaced desert.

Santa Bárbara, Changó marks the soles of women
born under Cuscatlán's veil, switching out ribbons
that try to bind any utterance with razor-edged
tongues so they can cut out every individual word.

Ay, pero esa Dolores traded in her knife
for a sandpaper stick from Thrifty's.
Smoothing the pointy, the jagged, she keeps
tabs on how many more coins
for two scoops of sweet.

Sitting with Estella, Dolores conjures
cumbias with sugar on top, about women
who aren't gonna take it anymore,
wishing rain on the parched pavement
she has settled on, taking stock of all the girlfriends
she'll need to call when her phone bill gets paid.

Cuchillera, you knife woman,
you will need this lesson
when your day begins and ends in this displaced desert.
No person, no amount of change
able to quench your thirst.

How to be Spiritual in Tacones

Practicing a prayer that bruises
ball and arch, I diagram step and movement
for the guy who thinks you can't be spiritual
in tacones. The dance jumps over dismissal,
wrestles the tragedy, slides under the mark
of the question, how to be, how to be spiritual.

Heresy claims hurled. Yet, my devotion refuses
your speculation, simply because I bite the apple,
swoon for art on a heel, want to arrive
at the ceremony, in my very best. Armor
and shine my cloak as we offer lament and gratitude.
How to be spiritual in stilettos? Brother, walk with me.

You are Here

1.

Flashing lights—dots on a map–beacon from nine hours of road.
Paper unrolls to the tempo of seventies tapes spooling song
from speakers mounted between the paneling and carpet hull
of a brown Chevy van. Swaying to the music that lies to me
as I sleep without a seat or a belt, I will always need to adjust
my straps. Straightening, my shoulders settle
for solace in the back of a Salvadoran hippie bus.

2.

North of naturally occurring arecaceae, an elongated area of wood floor
rolls out between the buzz of Mission Street and the palm of his hand
across her cheek. A Buddhist using tea bags and mantras to mend
a broken umbilical cord clarified for us, all of us, his mother
sitting upright in the old chair, my mother swiping away spirits,
my eleven-year-old-self, que él era el hombre, in charge—incase
there was a question. The good uncle looking for a new title
as he crumples a little girl's illusion that safe is somewhere.
How do you flatten the edges of an old photo, the urge to accept
the order of things? The woman did barge into his mother's house,
push past her too hard, yell in too high a pitch. Dark imprint of five
fingers on skin, the shadow tied our tongues. Watch how you
swing it, a man might force it back into place. Pursed lips holding
his cigarette, he only really needed one hand.

3.

The back roads of proud proclamations. Between black sand
conception, barrio migration—I cried first in Hollywood.
Years behind the freeway, sirens coloring the driveway

bearing dead dogs, murdered uncles, shaped my pilgrimage away
from dishonest trees promising vacation spots and movie stars
on the set of a desert. Movement prevents scar tissue, but footprints
don't erase birthmarks. How come you're not crazy, how,
well-meaning friends ask quietly, did you make it out alive?

4.
Phantoms beckon from a corridor of playground,
bus route, pupusa take out on Vermont and Melrose.
All threads along the knotted 101 rope of highway.
The promise of Santanecas that come in twos and
embossed San Francisco t-shirts chokes on typhoons
of yelled sentiment better left in discord; a debt
counting on short sweet reprieves like seals barking
below the cliff. The van parked—we all needed to sleep
in the back of the Salvadoran hippie bus.
Trusting wrinkled graphs of paper road to lead us
in the right direction, we discover the way home
as a colorful tapestry of detour and disaster.

Lotería de la mujer

La Adolescente y La Quinceñera
relate experience in acrylic and haiku.
La Vaga bites off only the verses
she can stomach, feeds from women,
like La Trabajadora, who speak
in simple truths, who drink La Madre
despite contagion and thorn.

La Enamorada dances descalza,
boasts a seismic laughter, wipes the fog
from la La Vuida's brow, holds
heart-to-hearts with La Muerte.
La Enamorada will shape her own mirrors.

La Bebe calls out the cards,
creates new sayings to rhyme
the reason de La Mujer and runs away
con las malditas cartas del juego.

¡Lotería!

Tinta

I origami secrets out of bone. Mother
tells me pray even though she doesn't always,
if she does, mostly it is out of costumbre.

Worry shakes like dice, serves sentences
on my irritated tongue. I bargain con el destino.

Brown black clumps of everyday accentuate
my mouth, thought bubble blurry,
lips hiding behind the shiny I wear—camouflage
for what fills my fists.

Little girl don't go outside something burning
in front of the door. Little girl, little girl in her belly.
Little girl can't buy pizza. Someone died there.
Little girl lives on same block all her life.
Little girl dancing hips, blooming hyacinths.
Little girl perspective wider than la calle.

Corners and crosswalks bounce off
my arms like fingers flicking. Tantas veces
he querido aplastarte la cara until my curves
and all black and many rings and tight and hair high
and attitude fade. What are you looking at?

The boom and bass of my defiance.
A nadie le importa. No one locks
the puertas to keep out spirits that touch me
wrong sometimes. Me meten plomo en el pelo.

The tinta colors in daughter discomfort, mother
curdling shoulder, little girl overflowing shame,
captures little girl throwing pencil at teacher
confused by new story endings she doesn't understand.

How to harvest the scar tissue of these blocks
collaged onto muchacha backbones?
No magazine spread can display the roots
of la calle sobre la piel. Tinta
runs down my cheek, the telling
sprints from my mouth
open, like a pincushion.

Bringing Up the Sun

The changing of the flag waves Central American
today. Church bells sit still over a tombstoned dawning.
Heading towards the sun beyond la Dolores, calle
named after pained bricks that hold Mission monuments
together, businesses that help you bury your dead, raise
your stripes, dominate the strip. Mortuaries abound,
doors wide open like the defeated mouth of a mother
who has lost her son.

No news breaks. Three quick facts on a back page,
devoid of desperate looks, gasps stopped
short—nobody of note. Nervous bravado
commands prodigal descendants of volcanic piedra,
once sacrificial daggers reduced to nonchalant weapon.
Brother competes against brother to bring the next day up.
Morning greets wringing hands, shaking heads gathering
for another entierro. Each new day
carrying heavier bags under its eyes.

Flattened metal versions of obsidian scratching out
our sons' storylines. So many translations of a boy
in the making, made like tiny rubber homie dolls
we spin out for fifty cents.
We salvage hope in the school yard,
where little brothers you can't get for two quarters
shake hands after getting mad, can't wait to go ice skating,
tell stories about 500-year-old grandfathers.

On the other side of bright blue school walls that give guise
to us, mortuaries fly flags for good business. Boys start asking
which set of colors belong to them. Stripes block
the light so false emblems sneak in, peddling allegiance,
sacrifice, in the form of our sons.

When I ask after the sun, the old man shrugs.
Es que no sé hija, the flag, the flag was in the way.

On the First Day of War,
I'm Supposed to Teach Poetry

Crumpled flyers hold up letters curling into small fists.
Declaring for fill in the blank geographic locations.

U.S. OUT OF...

Feet from far away once, rush past community center boards
avoiding announcements that bear down on the necks of nails.

Makeshift stands sell knock offs, represent various invasions,
military aided neighbors as Adams Morgan ushers in March 20th
under clouds bursting with contempt for us.

Fleeing the deluge in a Moroccan import store, a woman planted
here, words accented, hands in perpetual motion like my mother,
wants to know if I'm related, from similar places.

Her tone comforts and shames my fear we will be mistaken.
If they come in the morning, in case they come, she places copper
wishes for wearing around my wrists. I receive her recounting
of how she's come to own a small corner of transported smells,
walls layered with fabrics that hold her cuento,
I'm afraid, people are crazy, she confesses.

U.S. OUT OF...

Countries stand single file down the page. Long list of wrong time
wrong place nations pushing and shoving for their recognition

in the blank of t-shirt or button slogan. Like the ones teaching me
about back home, my points of reference: war broadcasts

and loud voices over a delayed signal. Long distance phone calls
hung over my childhood like a rain cloud moving. Rain back home,
my father would relate, came warm from the sky and traveled
as if it were running.

Like everyone is now, if, you look like the blank. If they come
in the morning, if they come, history will sleep in, lulled
by the refrain: not in my backyard. I could never take that
for granted accidental citizen of rain cloud empire
that is always running.

U.S. OUT OF...

The moment descends forming puddles behind my steps
down elementary school hallway. I have come to ask them
to write their life, but they need to mark the moment.
Eleven years writing, Michael manifests a boat
called hope that takes him nowhere; Reem
describes bumps falling from a desert sky;
Jamaal's rhymes remind us that in wars—people die.

March 20, 2003 brings a downpour of declarations
descending from the pens of sixth graders
who take role and check innocence absent.

U.S. OUT OF...

Can You Make a Fist

Circles past thirty, proof of identity
still required for a glass of spirits
over ice, for feet moving
in front of a live drum, for a cigar
meant to keep ánimas settled
even, faculty library book privileges,
yet chronic joint pain seeps
into my daily with no regard for my age

No deliverance from tingling fingers
crocheting this testimonio
despite interference, carpal cervical spinal
tie a dense cord around my neck
nerves in disorder disabling
my freedom to move my hands
rain clouds form rings around movement
ants wearing spiked heels dance on my forearms
knife wielding insect mobs
invade my instrument of expression, just
how history likes me, tongue tied and still
if I don't move, the pain is less

When called to take on
this form my spirit twisted,
warned creator that this one
comes full, so the pairing
sprung out stem and thorn,
fly and spider web

Press record on new gadget,
speak spite into speaker
if I can't write, I will say it,
prison house of my body
humbled by your tests,
my words are not resting
Raise your fist
U.S. ! OUT! OF!

Siguanaba

Con el agua del río, con el agua del mar
con el agua del río, yo me llevo todo el malo

The accounts from first countries
ring expectation in our ears
that girls who live at the river
arrive there in punishment.

Puzzle pieces of legend outline our paths,
tell tales about women needing
liberation from dirty, from choice, themselves.

Con el agua del río, con el agua del mar
con el agua del río, yo me llevo todo el malo

Water songs faint behind bus emissions, alongside women
pushing food, balancing babies, strutting bodies tattooed
with blanks waiting to be filled.

Water songs reshape shoulders cowering from myths
about bad mothers made ugly tasked
with spooking the misbehaving.

Have you heard
aunque la calle está sucia
and the trees are bitter,
Oshún vive aquí

River runs through the Mission by way of interlocking stories.
Lessons passed like batons in a race, like a drug exchange
with a nod, a pound—entre nosotras.

Have you heard
13, she runs track writes poetry and smiles hello
at the 45 years of a splintered heart woman
who rocks leyenda on her front porch
anticipating new endings 23 years
of sewing hands next door might bring her.
10, she spits words like too thick cloth
squeezing in between small gaps under doors
closed like her speech.
8, her raised hands jitter to help teacher.
29, teacher lost in unfinished sentences
shooting in the air—skinny five fingered branches.
35, squeezing water from long strands
she washes her hair in the sink
walks the river down the street
laughs at the man's verbal intrusions
fizzling mid-air, so starved for a medicine not for sale.
3, she practices swim strokes, plans to run track
maybe write poetry and smile hello
at the woman rocking leyenda on her front porch
about how the river isn't so bad.

Have you heard
aunque la calle está sucia
and the trees are bitter
Oshún vive aquí

The river flows blue and red from la muralista's brush,
stamping our likeness on the sides of buildings.
Reassuring us women's power, like that of water,
is feared, misunderstood,
even by gods.

Con el agua del río, con el agua del mar
con el agua del río, yo me llevo todo el malo

Canción misionera

En el distrito de la Misión, las flores crecen del concreto
los niños saltan de los volcanes
rebalsando de los callejones
las abuelas caminan con pan en las manos
y mi alma teje raíces sobre estas cuadras sagradas

Románticas amorous and painful on rotation
me pregunto, if you remember how we met.

Blank page of road, short and extended versions,
led me to you. A medley of sixties and seventies classics
filling the van as we pushed north—the closest
our little familia of three would get to a Chevy Chase vacation.

Hopscotch jumps from southern sprawl to tightly northern knit,
your walkable landscape safer than football field size blocks.
A place to count on, feel cool air on my temples, hunt
for marbles and ice cream on Mission.

Destitute, the ghosts followed. The grandfather
I barely met passed away an hour south. My father's father,
never lived in this country, but played billiards,
chalked late night Zócalo stories way before I did.

Shedding the familial epidermis, I learned to dance
con las ánimas at el Río when there were more folks,
less hipsters. Counting steps between numbered streets,
I have never lived on any block as long as I have here.

Erupting from the freeway, I wrapped my arms tight
around these painted city corners.

Asked the owl to deliver this report for me, scrawl it
in wet cement, leave it on coffee tables, so everyone
will know why I sing you románticas, amorous and painful.

Los evangelistas les gritan a las esquinas
los murales en las paredes se ríen en respuesta
en el distrito de la Misión, la gente baila sin pareja
*a su propio ritmo, a su propia manera**

Mi Gente (¡Ustedes!)

3

I believe the world is beautiful and that poetry, like bread is for everyone. And that my veins don't end in me but in the unanimous blood of those who struggle for life...

ROQUE DALTON

Chacarera de palabras

Si yo le pregunto al mundo,
el mundo me ha de engañar…

How to decipher songs embedded in ocean foam.
Your voice held poetry in its womb, incantations
fluttering on their own, only directions shifting,
remembering how broken hands didn't sever
Jara's cords.

Al ritmo de una chacarera te despediste, cantando.
¿Quién nos detendrá la piernas con canción,
cómo despertaremos del cansancio de lograr
por las multitudes, lo básico?

Tucumán, Argentina. 1935. First steps
into a moment when women in the world
were tuning their voices. Birthplace named
for the crossing of straw cords weaved together
like a chain, tied by songs sewing struggle into solidarity,
stitching the holes between strangers closed.

Madre de nuestro canto born six months after
a fearless woman to the north took flight
over a strip of smirking ocean, first
to test her reach between Oakland and Honolulu.
Women here, women there, connecting the dots, linked
by how willing they were to snub expectation, snap skin red.

Si no creyera en la balanza
en la razón del equilibrio…

Resplendent, her humility, burgeoning unsung legend,
stirring vibratos under Sistine chapel dome, holding
Carnegie Hall chairs captive, summoning flocks of listeners
to the Rome Coliseum. She sang loudest under candlelit
Mission district flats where community workers cooled heels
by the fire of cassette tapes, old guitars.

Tu voz fue nuestra guía, showing us to turn the mud
fertile, to plant defiance, grow silence into ballads.

Soñé que el río me hablaba…
…Tú que puedes, vuélvete

Decades of song settle like falling leaves, life saving
rhythms watering trunks, patient
for the valley of your voice to return.
Cautious birds listen for the wind chiming welcome:
Bienvenida, bienvenida cancionera.

Esta chacarera te ofrecemos para recordar,
preguntando que poemas nuevos fuiste a buscar.
Pedimos que nos sigas cantando del mar, de los cerros,
con los pájaros bailando en tu pelo.

Cante en paz, cante en paz, sing
in peace, Mercedes Sosa.

Tempest

E oya wimi loro e   oya kara orisha aleyo
e ki ma yoro   eke ola

Oya spins nets of steel around my shoulders,
choreographs piles of leaves, unlocks the cemetery,
sweeps through underground grates separating a chorus
of shuffling feet from public transport trains

Oya lifts up manholes, blasts her name in aerosol
across black bars that imprison spirits
under sidewalks crowded with the marching of muted melody

Oya opens the doors for the muertos, tears through metal,
plucks scarred petals, and through a hole in the ground
pulls me into a kaleidoscope of history spinning
the hands of one people pushing down
on the bent backs of all the rest

Oya filters my thoughts through an out of focus inquisition
of self, she asks me where are my ghosts, I get nervous
search through my bag, run home, ransack,
retrace steps, check messages, frantic, looking,
I miss them sitting next to concrete, trees whispering
at the waves of walkers spitting at their heels unwritten remnants,
selling bracelets that carry survival from far away
where labouring under wrinkled sun reflection, older sisters
sing homage to agua y tierra, remembering la gitana who walked
across time, unraveling thread back to the eye of the story,
finding the lessons inside the mouth of my mother before,

her mother, a tidal telling awaiting release scribbled
in old eyeliner pencils colored in with glittery markers,
question marks filling hungry notebooks
in the arms of our daughters

Old woman ripped out from sanctuary,
the image repeats, negative of an old home movie
jammed, flipping over and over, looking
back towards silk wishes of priestess-dom,
before thy kingdom come

oya de ariwo

Scanning the classifieds the ghost question
taunts, then I forget, miss the long-haired women
clad in white walking their mourning down the street
I am them I am her, bringing remembrance of warrior
made monster, I resist the void in the unspoken, so I say
everything loud because of 1 in 3
statistics scream, ghosts review ballistics
and like the sister who was not sorry
her brother was dead, my ghosts show me
not to regret

Searching, I follow circles
that lie dormant under undocumented eruptions,
pushing me back to the volcanoes of my parents' birthplace
that explode with the mark of birth on my leg

Ashe

Luna de Papel

Ya salió la luna
ya salió la luna
luz en mi cara
mi alma desnuda
Hay vienen los poetas
y las cantantes
vas a tener que contarles las penas

I tried to wrestle with the moon
y me mordió la lengua.

She pounded my poems into shards,
severing them. La luna se me metió
en la boca, pulling my tongue
for not being honest enough.

So I took up drawing, cut clothes out
for a paper doll. Teasing stories into
her pelo. La Poetisa, I call her,
loose strands tucked under pulp headwrap,
behind a griot mask. I painted it for her
to safely scavenge for aging books and hidden liner notes.

Ink on foot and finger y la calle her keyboard.
¡La vecindad! The neighborhood—la mera canción
that doesn't let the heart break. The refrain,
saludos to los revolucionarios, berets
teetering on their heads, sipping
nostalgia from ceramic mugs.

Los hermanos poetas yell metaphor,
stuff their angst into sermon. Las mujeres
craft medicine from liberated vocal chords.
La Poetisa strips the thorns from each
papier-mâché flower of a poem.

En la Misión, El Poeta Laureado embraces
the escritores he calls together to tie cantos
along la veinticuatro. Mission murals
diagram arteries and chi points. La Poetisa,
hides behind curtains of fog, watches

for Texidor to push his cane into the stars
turning on the sky so GGP can see when he shouts
out his window ¡abran los ojos cabrones! Lorna packs up
the waves, wheat pasting lines on the telephone poll.
Avotjca gets the call to bring the salve of her drum.

La Poetisa doles out frozen truths for you to lick
on a cold day. La memoria vuela
con las cuerdas del charango. I ask la luna
if I am made of paper, can I erase
the extranjeros building so high into the sky,
they block the stars on la veinticuatro.

hay vienen los poetas
y las cantantes
vas a tener que contarles las penas

La Poetisa distributes messages tied to her feet
landing at Galería to declarar
new poems under the full moon.
Everyone waiting. Filling the room

with our children now, small hands
keeping time, counting the years
when it was the poetry
that brought us together.

Ya salió la luna
ya salió la luna
luz en mi cara
mi alma desnuda
Hay vienen los poetas
y las cantantes
vas a tener que contarles las penas

Ranchera Re-mix

En México, it's not the water a spoiled
pocha stomach has to watch out for,
it's the rancheras.

Me gusta cantarle al viento...

La Manzanita holds her hands out when she
sings as if to embrace you, the notes,
stirring from her gut decorate the city's dusty air,
and even she needs a napkin
to wipe the melancholy haunting her canción.

No volveré, te lo juro por dios...

Expertly, she maintains black rings around her eyes
that track quiet pains in her chest, despedidas to all
the loves she's buried. The sting of father's pride,
so many false starts, the march around La Plaza Garibaldi
offering bitter reality in a sweet melody so she can get paid.

No tengo dinero ni nada que dar...

En México, it's not the threat
of whether your tourist ass will get jacked
by the taxi drivers that you have to watch, it's
the relentless canciones.

Soy basura tirada,
falsa mala y traicionera...

It's the relentless canciones
that make you wanna jump in front of a bicitaxi,
offer up your dismembered heart
in the place of La Coyolxauhqui,
that make you wanna holler, pull
the pinche car over, drama filling you from your head
to your patas, letting it out, unas ganas de gritar
MAAAAAAAAA-TEN-MEHHHH
Just. Kill. Me.

The animated version features super shero girls
donning slick outfits, cool spy glasses and cigars,
running through D.F.'s alleys smashing on men
who let stupidity unfurl too far from their mouths.
Chacamatrix platforms on their necks, cabrones
receive notification. No, we have no chaperones,
we do not ask for permission.

The Malinche tour provides the soundtrack
for our adventure. Las Siguanabas open
for las Hijas de la Chingada, they're covering
Lydia Mendoza.

Mal hombre, tan ruín es tu alma que no tiene nombre...

Salvation comes from the most unexpected
places. For us it was a country music loving
taxista with a soft spot for Queen.
He drove with his finger conducting in the air,
blasting Freddy Mercury down a lonely street.

Ma-maaa---ooo ooo ooo...

Getting out of the car, we called after our mama's too,
grateful for our survival. Not from the city, the water,
the taxis, but la catrina's corazón partido, that no one
can excavate, suffocating under the metro rail.

We witnessed the swollen organ with espinas
blocking full view of its secrets and wishes. We scribbled
notes on napkins, found clues under the rocks.
It wasn't ancient, her message. Didn't show us how to
wax on, wax off. It came out simple. It came out rough.

¡Ya! Ya no mamen con la maldita tristeza,
and please, will somebody please
turn the pinche radio off.

Flowers for My Fathers

Loroco, petal-less hybrid, some seed,
some herb, the translation of a different type of
skin, edible and tasteless. Izote, flor de comer,
its clustered white petals are a part of a system
no time for sitting in vases. We eat everything,
make order in the expanding raceme of reminiscence
by collecting scraps of ojas we can boil into food.

Abuelo used to send me booklets with perforated
images outlining classifications of plants that grew
above the soot, the practical izote bulbs, that complex
national flower. I cut the squares out
and glued them in place.

The plant's sharp leaves shaved off
words from the pencils the people hustle
but don't use. Gente who pretend to have.

Abuelo doesn't recognize the postcard he wants
to remember. Palmas line the loneliness, and behind
them, spirits scatter then succumb to the wind.
We explain to the air that luto weighs us down
seldom dissipates in this crowded cell.
So few of us left, he says.

His alma still witnesses the strange vegetation
and the avocados grow into the sky, in the middle
of the house, in time, despite the thorny threads

that hang from an unwinding origin. Black, warm
water conception does not make you

from here. I leave with a frayed shawl
clinging rough to my shoulders, and the raspy
voices that run in the family that calls me
daughter, tells me to carry handwritten recipes in my
throat—take care to not let them strangle.

Ruined

The largest pyramid ever built sits south, watching
over a city colonized by densely packed church towers.
Adobe temple steadfast in Cholula wearing the mountain
as mask, a cross as crown. Una Virgen adorned with trash.

A thirsty ruin adapts to soda can sips inside sanctuary. Sellers
every twenty steps marketing an array of drinks and nuts
distracting from the tire of the climb, the secrets
seeping from pretending to sleep piedras.

Countless steps slant towards the sky. A shiny
ornate yellow church charging for passage
between sacred ancient edifice and alivio.

Repurposed pyramid, dressed as nuestra Señora
de los Remedios, invites pilgrimage. Lit candles
send song to San Lázaro. Melodies conjure
the vending of excavation, the packaging of prayer.

Offerings of plastic bottles, soiled paper, basura
drip down mountainside. Waste disregards pyramid
built as refuge from water overcoming the valley.
This Señora in charge of distribution
doles out relief reluctantly.

Behind a narrow doorway, bartender holds down
corner cantina, barters integrity for forgiveness,
no beer para el borracho buscando solo una más.

El hombre stumbles his defeat
towards the whistle of los voladores.

At the foot of the biggest pyramid men hang
upside down, fly their ceremony in four,
five directions of fluted yearnings.
Elaborate ritual: explained, justified, billed.
Men fly for donation, for a creator who won't mind
that they sell their ceremony to get by.

Tlachihualtepetl. Artificial Mountain
holding plastic prayers prepared to ascend.
El borracho won't climb the pyramid, a church
on its head, pretends instead, arms open, to fly there.

La diosa del parque

Grass but no trees under buzzing traffic
where sidewalks radiate rainbows on windshields.
A park where pyramids stage children dancing their history,
splashing color, pasting leaves onto the landscape as cars
speed past, trade street and sky without hearing a gente's pride
bounce up from animal skin.

Serpent skirt deity holds up the road, a vandal
sprays her red. Angry that she won't wear make-up,
frightened by her lipstick free confidence. Just angry.
Just frightened.

La comunidad formando un círculo
sobre unas cuantas cuadras de Barrio Logan
por un día, en la primavera.

During this gathering every April, the tide swells,
an ocean of hues, sand, caramelo, chocolate flows
under the freeway. One day out of three hundred
and sixty five when we see, when we hold
ourselves.

One Million Minus One

Qué viva la memoria y el espíritu de Anthony Soltero

Me cortaron la lengua, pero tengo mis pies

Millions marching mimeograph
our caras onto international view.
No caption does justice to the sight.
If they take your tongue, well
you still have your feet.

The headline of the mass outpouring
of raised voices and fists invoke Judy Baca.
Staggered portraits along the river, palms
open, holding light. Al fin, murals and gente
hiding debajo del horizonte emerge
in a blazing, deliberate chant.

Rally cries can't muffle a mother's llanto.
Her son walked to the front, raised
his chin. An administrator pulled him
out of line. Leaned too heavy
on tentative boy backbone.
The traverse toward manhood stunted.

Mother's arms flail around the empty space
where awkward middle school limbs played
with equilibrium, tested reach, resistance.
A rubber band that snapped.

Por qué es que han marcado una línea en la tierra
por qué es que han creado la escuela como cárcel
estudiantes criminales, los maestros policías
Me cortaron la lengua, pero tengo mis pies

Belated obituary won't pull chalk
out of the hands of boys drawing their outlines,
their surrender, onto the sidewalk.

The absence of news coverage
about a principal who slipped
the bolt out from a boy's spine,
the clatter of bone as he retreated
into the comfort of district policies,
won't erase the occurrence,
the date, the time.

Este pedacito de hombre, why
did he take a principal's threat
like a gun to his head?
Didn't anyone tell him, regardless
of how teachers menace,
accusations stick, skin reflects,

you are precious.
You are precious.
You are precious.

What the Water Gave Me

Yemayá assessu
she opens her hands
assessu Yemayá
washes salt over my belly
Yemayá olodo
hija única, only daughter,
it's your time to carry this

the first born es un pétalo despertando
el pensamiento, la promesa de la primavera,
de primeros amores, del primer hijo, el hilo
de la esperanza

my first born grows into promises of grace,
singing new seasons, spawning new visions
of what I can look like, esperándolo,

I carry the weight forming, feeling heavy
like a good morning heartache verse
punctuating the air, heavy like piano keys
in a crescendo falling onto the shores of our listening,

heavy like pockets full of posies,
and I fall down, pockets full
of pennies, too many two cent offerings
scribbled onto rubber band of skin

preference prediction pronounce
if you have nausea, you're having a girl
because girls make you sick

gurrl, you're soo big
esa barriga, yells the woman
with a big barriga of her own, ay, sí,
you're having a girl
or a boy, strangers
at the market, on the street
lay hands, offer opinions

I unwrap banana leaves of my own ideas
of when you'll come, how you'll sing

trying to avoid for now that my caterpillar
will be a girl, or boy carrying
swords or tea cups

swimming from the intersection
of Yemayá's tide, Oshun's stream,
past the markers awaiting your arrival,
don't mind the windows padded with white
ruffled icing dresses, look for the fruit trees

packed in boxes, adorning street corners,
shipwrecked remnants of yesterday's cena
floating under Mission trees because nothing

should be wasted, confetti from festivals past
strewn along your path, guiding you,
roses red growing tall
over the shoulders of señoras

look for closets spilling out of windows,
laundry bursting from bags, truck beds
carrying more things, more bodies

than can fit, working arms moving faster
than they should, all sign posts to find

your way home, and don't bring shells
unless you leave pennies
for Yemaya don't bring songs
unless you sing
for la Virgen de la Caridad

as you swing I sew songs for you
Esta mariposa
vuela vuela vuela
I imagine as a girl
you'll look at me with his eyes
laugh loud when you play with swords
baila con el viento se ríe del guerrero
as a boy you'll smile with my eyes
pedacito de mi piel de mi corazón
tell me boys can be butterflies too

Corazón

I am growing brothers. Underneath the elastic
holding up occupied muscle, a renewed span
of bosom bounces baby boy
in waiting, extending limbs. His older brother
describes the movement of small growing
fists denting my skin,
like a flutter, an absolute heartbeat.

Five-year-old hands rub my tired back, sing high
pitched songs landing a soft bell in my ear.
I'm trying to rewrite the lyrics, pending.

When we meet, baby boy,
you will require explanation
about the first of my grey hairs, about why
the lullabies I swaddle you in are a privilege,
why so many babies cry in cribs, desperate for song,
that your father's poems give me the strength
to bear you into a world with little floor beneath us.

You will swim, rub away tiny scars
marking my spine stretched from carrying you,
understand the nets I hold together
for other people's children—my children too.
You will recognize this clash of asphalt, idiomas,
transposed tropical food, vagos poetas, as a perfect
picture of the place where we are home.

You will steady even when the weight tries to tip you
with bricks your brother will learn to lift first, posture
slanted by newly ordered letters of your names,
expectations of your not quite regular skin, assumption
that you must come from farther away, that you are entertainer,
not intellectual. You will learn to dodge. You will have to float.

We will thank the water, talk
to the rocks, and make petitions to the crows.
Every day we will draw until our pictures spill
over the edges of the paper. Concocting colors that can
make sense of the backdrop on the other side of our sleeping,
I will have to confess that babies don't all have
blankets, that some boys disappoint their mothers,
that some mothers are too desperate to hold their sons, that in
different parts of the world bombs bring the morning
and the distance is shrinking, that our family
lived in one of those far away places, that we are not one language
or one people, but many and the distance
is shrinking.

What I won't have to explain
is that in our small apartment,
painted by the warmth of our laughter,
your brother is talking and drawing
in twos now. Your father is carving letters
for your name. I am crafting songs
to receive you into this imperfect picture
of a place we call home
where we wait for you.

Despierta

Mission Street yawns wide under the canopy of breaking day,
breathless footsteps tax rickety ladder rungs,
chase streams of light unveiling the horizon,
sleepy hands burning sage on tar rooftop,
the day just barely born
into my desert dusted arms wanting
to hold a neighborhood hostage from itself

What a perfect mission these streets have become,
shoveling out plots for graves, lots for sale
a concentric circle of conquest carving itself
into a ground overcrowded with the whispering of ghosts

If I charge the children with painting poems,
will you learn to feed yourself, curl up from the crouching
towards death stance you slag around the streets in,
cease the fire that barrels holes through the heads
of young men guilty of nothing but brown skin,
being on foot—no car to speed past the candle lit
processing of their own untimely deaths

La piedra del sol down la calle Valencia reflects
light from a Chicana architect's plans, shines
over open doors of a community learning space,
comedores bearing plates steaming with home country
recuerdos, connecting writers to the next verse,
amantes to inevitable missteps

Prayers printed on the feet of danzantes resound
through blocks where I learned how to make crying count,
counted murals counting wars cried close to corners
where someone keeps dying for nothing, nodded
while poet cantos sing truth into sense
calling each day to attention with the promise
of sunrise and sanctuary

notas

To hear audio versions of selected poems, listen:
https://www.reverbnation.com/leticiahernandezlinares

Visit: joinleticia.com to buy the Mucha Muchacha c.d. (with artwork by Ana Teresa Fernández) and to learn more about my interdisciplinary performance projects.

Opening epigraph from the song "Alfonsina y el mar," sung by Mercedes Sosa and written by Félix Luna and Ariel Rámirez.

Comadre

Epigraph from Gioconda Belli's poem, "Madre mía de las palabras."

"Learning to Talk"
"Can You Feel the Beat" Lisa Lisa and the Cult Jam.

"Iba o" Yoruba song dedicated to the orisha who guards the crossroads, Eleguá.

"Too Much Girl"
For Marie and Mytili and Papo (because we took a different road).

"Amor en el tiempo boca abajo"
For Tomás.

"Porque no todos somos iguales"
Title borrows a line from the song "Desapariciones" by Rubén Blades.

I first performed this poem at Intersection of the Arts in San Francisco, in 2002. I created a small installation of an altar of names. I placed nametags on all the chairs in the venue, and encouraged audience members to offer names to the altar.

"Tragedilandia"
In remembrance of the victims of the 2001 earthquake(s) in El Salvador.

"Yo vengo de la tierra" (original song).

"Translating the Wash"
For Doris.

"Sweat"
Quote from *Tres Banderas*, litografía, 1988, by Juan Sánchez.

"Cumbia de salvación"
Words in italics are sung; most are samples or twists of the song "Sabrosa Cumbia" by Marito Rivera y su Grupo Bravo.

Hija

Epigraph from A *Daughter of Isis: The Autobiography of Nawal El Saadawi.*

"Shuco"
Atol is a warm cornmeal drink. Shuco is an atol made from black corn and served with black beans and ground pumpkin seeds.

"Lotería de la mujer"
After Nuvia Crisol Ruland's *Lotería de la Mujer.*
Visit http://www.artecrisol.com to view the Lotería or to purchase a Lotería greeting card and send one to someone you have a feeling for.

"Siguanaba"
After Juana Alicia's mural *La Llorona's Sacred Waters.*

To view the mural, visit the Mission District. The mural covers the wall on 24th and York Street. You can view images of the mural at http://www.juanaalicia.com/la-llorona-project-san-francisco/

Sigua-naba means "spirit" and "woman" in Nahuatl. The myth of La Siguanaba has several versions throughout Central America. One Salvadoran version tells of a young woman, Sihuehuet, who was punished by the rain god, Tlaloc, for being vain and for being a bad mother. She was renamed La Siguanaba and punished by being made ugly and a servant. She was sent to the river to lament her new monstrousness and scare drunken husbands and misbehaving children. She was also nicknamed the "Dirty One," hence her need to wash, clean, bathe. ¡Long live the dirty girls!

To read more about Juana Alicia's mural, pick up a copy of *Street Art San Francisco, Mission Muralismo*, edited by Annice Jacoby, and read my piece, "Painting the River Clean," pg. 39.

"Con el agua…" is a refrain from un espiritual cubano (Cuban Spiritual Song).

"Canción misionera"
Written for the 40th Anniversary of *El Tecolote Newspaper.*

Mi Gente (Ustedes!)

The title of this section invokes the song "Mi gente," by Héctor Lavoe: "Mi gente. ¡Ustedes!/lo más grande de este mundo/siempre me hacen sentir/un orgullo profundo."

Epigraph from Roque Dalton's *Poemas Clandestinos/Clandestine Poems.*

"Chacarera"
Chacarera: Argentinian folk music and dance.

Samples of songs often performed by Mercedes Sosa: "Guitarra Dímelo Tú" written by Atahualpa Yupanqui; "La Maza" written by Silvio Rodriguez; "Tú que puedes, vuélvete" written by Atahualpa Yupanqui.

"Tempest"
"E oya" Yoruba song for Oya, the orisha who rules the wind, associated with sudden change; a warrior spirit that stirs things up.

When I wrote this poem, the National Center for Victims of Crimes estimated 1 out of every 3 North American women would be sexually assaulted in her lifetime.

"Luna de papel"
Written on the 10th Anniversary of La Lunada Reading Series at Galería de la Raza, in the Mission District, San Francisco.

"Ya salio la luna" (original song).

Lines from this poem can be on viewed on the mural: *This Place: A Tribute to Calle 24*, located on Folsom and 24th Street, in the Mission District, San Francisco. The mural was directed by Precita Eyes muralists, Fred Alvarado and Max Martilla, and painted and designed by the Urban Youth Arts Program.

To read about the mural:
http://eltecolote.org/content/en/arts_culture/new-mural-captures-spirit-of-the-mission/

"Ranchera Re-mix"
Samples of rancheras include songs by: Chucho Monge; Antonio Aguilar; Juan Gabriel; Paquita la del Barrio; and Lydia Mendoza. Oh, there is one by Queen, too.

"La diosa del parque"
For Xican@ Park in Barrio Logan, San Diego. In honor of Tommie Camarillo. To learn more about Chicano Park, the historic place and events visit: http://chicano-park.org/

"One Million Minus One"
On March 30, 2006, 14-year-old Anthony Soltero, shot himself through the head after the assistant principal at De Anza Middle School in Ontario, California warned Anthony that he would go to prison for organizing protests and walk-outs in response to anti-immigrant legislation.

"Me cortaron la lengua" (original song).

The Judy Baca mural referenced here is the *Great Wall of Los Angeles*. This mural happens to be located in close proximity to where I lived during my high school years. I discovered the mural in my senior year of college during a slideshow in a Chicano Studies course (I recognized the park above it). #AccessisKey #EthnicStudies

To see the mural visit the *Great Wall of Los Angeles* on Coldwater Canyon. You can also view the mural: http://sparcinla.org/programs/the-great-wall-mural-los-angeles/

"What the Water Gave Me"
For Mahcic.

"Yemayá" Yoruba song for la madre who rules the ocean and all living things. ¡Omío Yemayá!

"Esta mariposa" (excerpt from original song).

"Corazón"
For Serafín.

gracias

Thanks to the editors and publications that have previously published these poems (some in different forms):

Chicana/Latina Studies: The Journal of MALCS: "Underneath the Cuento" and "Holy Mother" and "You are Here"; *La Lunada:* "Learning to Talk,"; *Crab Orchard Review:* "Sweat"; *The Other Side of the Postcard:* "Porque no todos somos iguales,"; *U.S. Latino Literature Today:* "Cumbia de Salvación"; *Huizache:* "Shuco"; *Acentos Review:* "La Cuchillera"; *Hinchas de Poesía:* "Luna de Papel" and "Ranchera Re-mix"; *Tea Party Magazine:* "Tempest."

What an honor it is to join Tía Chucha Press. My discovery of Luis Rodriguez's work certainly helped me arrive here. Appreciation to the press, al estimado Luis Rodriguez, y a la hermana Liana Cabrera, the newest members of my dream team.

For the incredible editorial equipo: Tomás Riley, Lorna Dee Cervantes, Dr. Deborah Paredez, Dr. Consuelo Mona Manríquez, Ángel García, Carmen Giménez Smith and Ire'ne Lara Silva.

For the privilege to use such a stunning cover image and for a fruitful and long time partnership: Ana Teresa Fernández. For always showing me in the best light, for photographic brilliance: Michelle Gutiérrez.

For community and inspiration: Rubén Martínez, devorah major, Rose Arrieta, Juana Alicia, Opal Palmer Adisa, Genny Lim, Janice Mirikitani, Ester Hernández, Olga Talamante, Alejandro Murguía, Jorge Argueta, Nancy Hom, Avotcja Jiltonilro, Jack Hirschman, Jaime Cortez, Sandra García Rivera, Galería de la Raza, Intersection for the Arts, The San Francisco Arts Commission, my neighborhood and community of 20 years, the

Mission District of San Francisco. Celeste Mendoza, Norma Cantú, Carmen Tafolla, Barbara Curiel, Naomi Ayala, Luivette Resto, Juan Luis Guzmán, Laurie Ann Guerrero, Millicent Accardi, Javier Zamora, Yesenia Montilla, and all my CantoMundo circle.

For mi familia, both born and chosen: Mi abuelo, Mama, and my hard working, inspiring parents, Leticia del Carmen and Carlos Ricardo. My siblings and co-conspirators: Raquel Gutiérrez and Robert Karimi. Y a mis tres amores, Tomás, Mahcic Emilio y Serafín Izal, thank you for understanding and loving and holding this mucha muchacha.